RELIGIONS OF HUMANIT

DATE DUE

FOLLETT

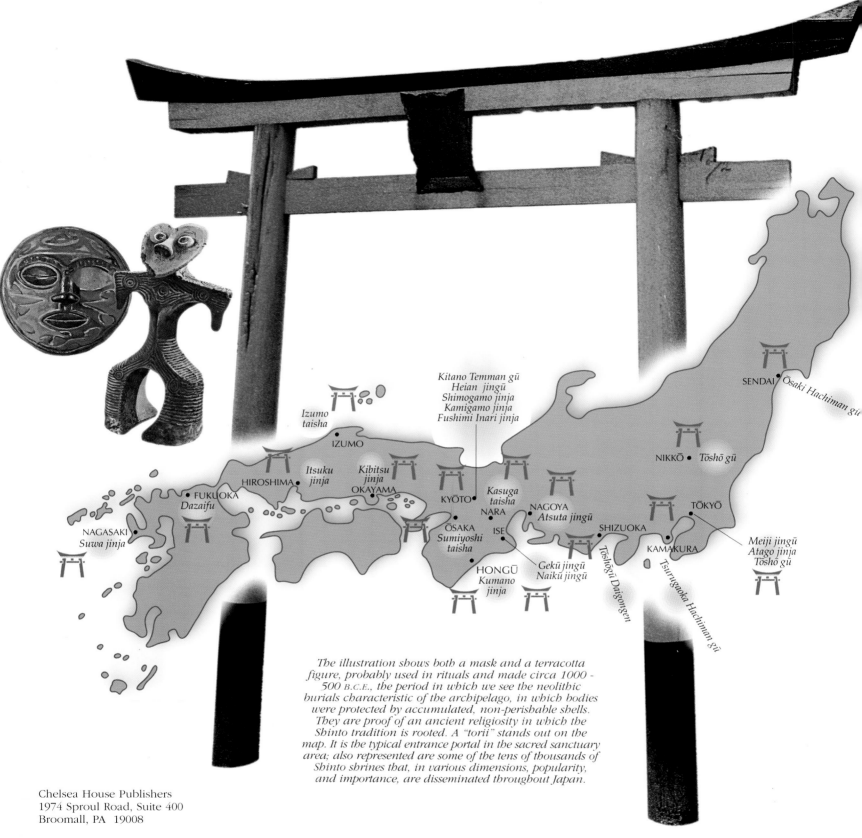

Kitano Temman gū
Heian jingū
Shimogamo jinja
Kamigamo jinja
Fushimi Inari jinja

SENDAI · Ōsaki Hachiman gū

Izumo
taisha

IZUMO

NIKKŌ · Tōshō gū

Itsuku
jinja

Kibitsu
jinja

HIROSHIMA ·

OKAYAMA

Kasuga
taisha

FUKUOKA ·
Dazaifu

KYŌTO

NARA

NAGOYA
Atsuta jingū

TŌKYŌ

NAGASAKI
Suwa jinja

ŌSAKA
Sumiyoshi
taisha

ISE

SHIZUOKA

KAMAKURA

Meiji jingū
Atago jinja
Tōshō gū

HONGŪ
Kumano
jinja

Gekū jingū
Naikū jingū

Tōshōgū Daigongen

Tsurugaoka Hachiman gū

The illustration shows both a mask and a terracotta figure, probably used in rituals and made circa 1000 - 500 B.C.E., the period in which we see the neolithic burials characteristic of the archipelago, in which bodies were protected by accumulated, non-perishable shells. They are proof of an ancient religiosity in which the Shinto tradition is rooted. A "torii" stands out on the map. It is the typical entrance portal in the sacred sanctuary area; also represented are some of the tens of thousands of Shinto shrines that, in various dimensions, popularity, and importance, are disseminated throughout Japan.

Chelsea House Publishers
1974 Sproul Road, Suite 400
Broomall, PA 19008

The Chelsea House
world wide web address is
www.chelseahouse.com

English-language edition
© 2002 by Chelsea House Publishers,
a subsidiary
of Haights Cross Communications
All rights reserved.

First Printing

1 3 5 7 9 6 4 2

Library of Congress Cataloging-
in-Publication Data Applied For:
ISBN: 0-7910-6631-2

© 2001 by
Editoriale Jaca Book spa, Milan
All rights reserved.
Originally published by
Editoriale Jaca Book, Milan, Italy

Design by Jaca Book

Original English text by
Lawrence E. Sullivan

function as a focus of worship in a shrine and allow for a direct encounter between the faithful and the *kami* to whom the shrine is dedicated. Emperors, and sometimes deified ancestors or heroes, have also occasionally been identified as *kami*. Finally, *kami* are linked with ideals, concepts, and abstractions. Even where *kami* are associated with built spaces such as shrines, they are not always considered permanent residents, but rather as transient beings, called down for special occasions and sent away after receiving offerings and prayers. Over the centuries, people have described how *kami* might take possession of animals (such as foxes or badgers) and even domestic pets like dogs and cats. These animals, in turn, when empowered by the *kami*, might take possession of human beings. An *ujigami* (somewhat like a household or family god) is a deity associated with a group of related kin, who once resided in the same village (*ujiko*).

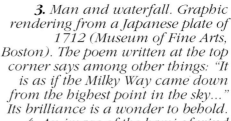

3. Man and waterfall. Graphic rendering from a Japanese plate of 1712 (Museum of Fine Arts, Boston). The poem written at the top corner says among other things: "It is as if the Milky Way came down from the highest point in the sky..." Its brilliance is a wonder to behold.
4. An image of the kami of wind and thunder kept in a Kyoto shrine, graphically rendered. It exemplifies the fact that natural phenomena and beauty or even human beings of irresistible exceptionality could signal the presence of kami— something that surpasses the human condition.

5. Oil painting (19th century) by an unknown artist, kept in the Constitutional Court Palace in Rome. Here one sees reiterated the ancient gesture, still in use today, of hanging prayers written on folded pieces of paper on a tree. In this way, the tree is recognized for its participation in a sacred environment.

13

4

EARLY SHINTO AND ITS BUDDHIST INFLUENCE

1. Graphic rendering from a woodcut (19th century). Amaterasu, solar divinity, is caught in the act of leaving the cave where she was hiding, offended by the violence of her brother Susano-o. Without her all was darkness. The other divinities tried to make her return, until they succeeded in enticing her out of the cave and the sunlight returned.

Shinto has changed over time, especially due to contact with religions originating outside Japan. In Japanese records of the eighth century, the principle *kami*, called *ujigami*, protected each clan and its territory. Sometimes, the *ujigami* was a divine, life-giving ancestor who founded the clan. When the nation unified under the imperial clan, its founding deity and ancestress, Amaterasu-O-Mi-kami, became worshipped beyond the imperial family palace. Myths about Amaterasu, among other matters, were gathered by Emperor Temmu (672-687 C.E.) and set down in writing soon afterward: the *Kojiki*, "Record of Ancient Matters," dating to 712 C.E, and the *Nihon Shoki*, "Chronicles of Japan," dating to 797 C.E., were both written in Chinese characters. Between the eighth and twelfth centuries (the early Heian Period), Shinto shrines were organized into a national system, based partly on native Japanese practices and partly on Chinese models. In 927 C.E., the *Engishiki* appeared in 50 volumes, including ten books on

rules and prayers for Shinto shrine organizations and ceremonies. For example, the *Daijo-sai*, the Great Thanksgiving, was celebrated during the enthronement of a new emperor and gifts of new cloth—changes of ceremonial clothing—were offered to the imperial ancestor *kami* at the onset of each summer and winter. To this day, Shinto reflects its association with groups, such as the clan, the village, the corporation, and the nation.

Early Shinto leaves little evidence of permanent shrines. *Kami* were believed to visit ritual sites near rivers, mountains, trees, or remarkable stones and to leave afterward. Later, permanent structures sheltered devotees and housed *kami* and their *goshintai*. Early shrines resembled rice granaries. To learn the will of the *kami*, ancient Japanese studied patterns of lines on tortoise shells or cracks on the burnt shoulder bones of deer. They received the *kami's* messages in dreams and trances of possession, when *kami* were believed to enter them.

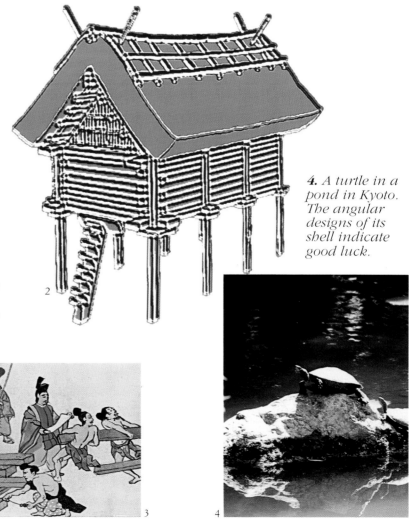

4. A turtle in a pond in Kyoto. The angular designs of its shell indicate good luck.

2. Reconstructed granary on stilts, introduced from China in the 3rd century B.C.E. Such buildings were probably used as models for the early Shinto shrines.
3. Construction workmen at work. Illustration from a scroll (14th century C.E.) that narrates the foundation of a sanctuary.

Engishiki, a tenth century collection. The *kami* are honored and entertained with music and dance. *Matsuri* festivals typically combine solemnity with merrymaking. Varieties of entertainment can involve horse racing, mountain climbing, log rolling, *sumo* wrestling, parades with floats, archery contests, and tugs-of-war, singing, drum ensembles, and masquerades. Prayers are offered by the general population, who often place branches of the *sakaki* tree before the *kami*. When the offerings are removed and the *kami* restored to its original place, the doors are closed again. The chief priest offers a last prayerful greeting and the ceremony ends. Then the festival meal (*naorai*) starts. In ancient times, the *naorai* meal was a special communion between *kami* and worshippers. The food, given to the *kami*, shared in their power. By eating it, devotees absorbed the *kami's* power into their own bodies. This sense of communion is still preserved in the plentiful drinking of *sake* at *matsuri* and in the Thanksgiving feasts carried on in the imperial household and in some shrines.

5

6

5. *Two sumo wrestlers in a Hokusai print (circa 1790). In Japan sumo wrestling is a rather popular sport whose roots are linked to the struggle between great mythological forces. In the sumo matches, the wrestling arena is purified and a series of ritual gestures opens the bouts, which often accompany festivals.* **6.** *The people in the illustration are ready to dive into the sea for a purifying immersion, a symbol of renewal connected to the Shinto celebration of the New Year.* **7.** *In the old section of Kyoto, in front of a small shrine, the lanterns are lit. These lanterns are always present during the festivals, and are a beacon of the clear integrity required of every person.*

7

9
TRANSFER OF THE SUN DEITY AT ISE

1. 2. In the bay of Ise two rocks evoke the divine primordial couple. Appearing after several stages of creation, they concerned themselves with the formation of the earth, and the origins of the archipelago and the kami of the sun, Amaterasu. The sun deity Amaterasu sent her nephew to reign in Japan. According to ancient mythology, the imperial dynasty descends from him.

6. Red cedar ("Cryptomeria japonica") forms vast forests in Japan. Its wood is used for the main buildings in the Ise shrine.
7. A complex ceremonial moment takes place at Ise in the course of periodic reconstructions.

3. 4. 5. A mirror, a jewel, and a sword: three treasures of Shinto ritual. Gifts from Amaterasu to her nephew, the first two enticed her out of the cave in which she hid. The sword is a symbol of struggle. Here we see from circa 300 B.C.E. a bronze mirror, a necklace with tiger-claw stones, and a seven pointed steel sword, which is the most ancient imperial symbol.

A special focus of Shinto life can be found at the three national Grand Shrines (*jingu*), of Izumo, Atsuta, and Ise, a town on Ise Bay. All year long, pilgrims stream to Ise from all over Japan to pay respects to Amaterasu, the sun deity, who is enshrined there. She is the founding ancestress of the Japanese imperial family. The Ise Grand Shrine is commonly regarded as the most ancient shrine in Japan, said to have originated in the mythic era, when the earth was new. Archaeology reveals that the innermost shrine at Ise existed as early as the third century; and the outer shrine dates at least to the fifth century. They are completely rebuilt every 20 years. The task is enormous, for some two hundred

8. *Ideogram of the word "norito," which indicates the ritual Shinto prayers, endowed with a noble style and an enchanted rhythm. The priest who directs the celebration recites such prayers based on ancient models at every festival.*

9. *In the woodcut by Hokusai: a shrine where devotion to the moon is being practiced, probably directed toward the brother of Amaterasu, Susano-o, who was banished from heaven for his misdeeds. Later Susano-o was redeemed and became the deity of the moon.*

9

buildings are remade, as are their ritual implements and ornaments. The refashioning cultivates traditional arts and crafts in each generation.

Toward the close of each 20-year period, ceremonies and pilgrimages multiply. Thousands of pilgrims in ceremonial garb may be seen hauling in white stones to pave the new building sites. The ritual activities of the *Shikinen Sengu* culminate in a solemn nighttime ritual, when Amaterasu-O-Mi-kami, with her ritual objects, is transferred from her old to her new home. Shrouded within a portable enclosure of white cloth, surrounded by torchbearers, and accompanied by priests playing eerie sounds on ancient musical instruments, Amaterasu slowly moves to her new quarters.

Her image is never seen, for it is transported as a reflection in a covered mirror and never brought into open view. During the ancient times described in myth, the *kami* used a mirror to coax the sun deity from the cave where she had withdrawn into hiding, plunging the world into darkness. She came forth to see her own reflection. The mirror and the sounds of the celebrating *kami* enticed the life-giving sun deity to re-enter the world. The mirror at Ise, reflecting the unseen Amaterasu, is a mystery wrapped in an enigma: even as it emerges from the old shrine to make the several-hundred-yard journey to the next abode, it remains covered and closed in a container, which, in turn, is ringed round with a white cloth.

A RITUAL PRAYER

HIRANO FESTIVAL
("Hirano no matsuri")

By command of the Emperor,
I humbly speak in the solemn presence
Of the Great Sovereign Deity
Who has been brought hither from Imaki and worshipped:

In accordance with your desires, oh Great Sovereign Deity,
In this place, The shrine posts
Have been broadly set up in the bedrock below,
The crossbeams of the roof
Soaring towards the High Heavenly Plain[1]
And [a shrine] established as a heavenly shelter,
As a sun-shelter,
And I (office, rank, surname, and name)
Of the Office of Rites,
Having been designated as "kamu-nusi"[2]
Do present the divine treasures:
Bows, swords, mirrors, bells,
Silken awnings, and horses have been lined up in rows;
Garments of colored cloth, radiant cloth,
Plain cloth, and coarse cloth have been provided;
The first fruits of the tribute presented
By the lands of the four quarters have been lined up:
The wine, raising high the soaring necks
Of the countless wine vessels filled to the brim;
The fruits of the mountain fields-
The sweet herbs and the bitter herbs-
As well as the fruits of the blue ocean-
The wide-finned and the narrow-finned fishes,
The seaweeds of the deep
And the seaweeds of the shore-
All these various offerings do I place, raising them high
Like a long mountain range, and present.
Receive, then, tranquilly, I pray, these noble offerings;
Bless the reign of the Emperor as eternal and unmoving,
Prosper it as an abundant reign,
And grant that he may abide for a myriad ages.
[Thus praying] I fulfill your praises
Thus I humbly speak.

Also I humbly speak:
Guard, I pray, the princes of the blood, the princes,
The courtiers, and the many officials here assembled
Who serve [the Emperor];
Guard them in the guarding by night
And the guarding by day,
And grant that they may serve in the Emperor's court
Ever higher, ever wider, always prospering
Like luxuriant, flourishing trees.
[Thus praying] I fulfill your praises
Thus I humbly speak.

[1] "High Heavenly Plain" refers to *takam-no-hara*, where the heavenly *kami* live, a world different from the visible world of human beings.
[2] The *kamu-nusi* is the title of the Shinto priest who is in charge of ceremonial life at a shrine and performs certain ceremonies. Today he is called *kannushi*.

An imperial messenger recited this ritual prayer (*norito*) at the Hirano shrine in Kyoto during the fourth and eleventh months of the year. The prayer and offerings were made to a *kami* brought to Hirano from the town of Imaki. The *kami* is asked to bless the Imperial Court with peace, health, and abundant long life. Recorded during the tenth century, such *norito* continue to serve as models for Shinto prayer today.